CHRISTMAS KALEIDOSCOPE

arranged by Robert S. Frost

The Collection

CHRISTMAS KALEIDOSCOPE is a collection of well-known Christmas carols. This book has been arranged so that each instrument has the melody line as well as additional harmony lines. Many instrument combinations are possible from small chamber ensembles to a large string orchestra. With the addition of the piano, any size string group can perform these selections with success on holiday programs.

Available for Violin, Viola, Cello, String Bass, Piano and Full Score.

KJOS NEIL A. KJOS MUSIC COMPANY • SAN DIEGO, CALIFORNIA

Contents

ISBN 0-8497-3211-5

Jolly Old St. Nicholas

trad. American carol

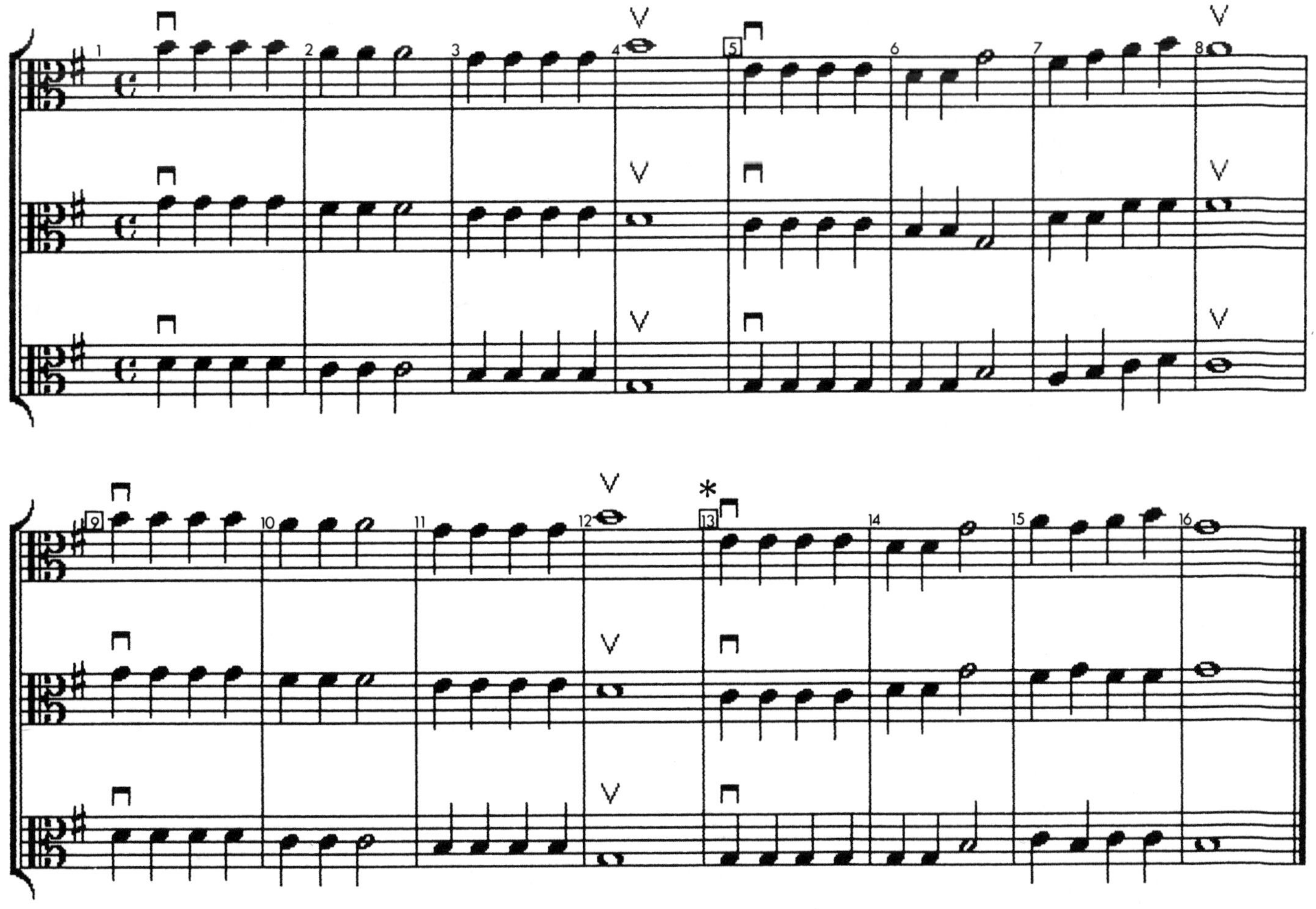

*Introduction

Good King Wenceslas

old English carol

Adeste Fideles

anonymous

The Infant King

Polish carol

Up on the Housetop

B.R. Hanby

We Wish You a Merry Christmas

trad. English carol

We Three Kings

John H. Hopkins

Away in a Manger

James Ramsey Murray

Hark! the Herald Angels Sing

Felix Mendelssohn

The First Noel

old French carol

Angels We Have Heard on High

trad. French carol

God Rest Ye Merry Gentlemen

old English carol

Deck the Halls

old Welsh air

Joy to the World

G.F. Handel